Willis Smith, early park naturalist, 1934

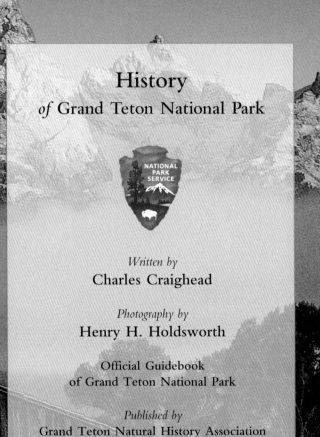

History
of Grand Teton National Park

Written by
Charles Craighead

Photography by
Henry H. Holdsworth

Official Guidebook
of Grand Teton National Park

Published by
Grand Teton Natural History Association

Table *of* Contents

John Moulton's Mormon Row homestead (1916) today

People in the Landscape

The history of this place we call Grand Teton National Park comes to us in several ways—as a collection of moments from the past written on paper and preserved in photographs, as stories retold, customs passed down, and as physical objects that have survived over the intervening years. Through them we paint a picture of what happened, what people's lives were like, and how they fit into this landscape. The farther back we look, the fewer of those moments remain for us to study and the less detail we know. In this park, the human history covers 12,000 years, but we have written records for only two percent of that span, from about 1800 A.D. on. Without diminishing the importance of the vast prehistoric era, it is necessarily the more recent times and people that have a greater bearing on this place as a national park. But ironically, it is a philosophy of respect for the land inherent in the American Indian cultures throughout history that shapes the National Park Service land use policies today.

It wasn't until the homesteading era that permanent structures began to dot the landscape, records were kept, and the day-to-day details of culture were preserved. This is when we begin to see the unfolding of a community philosophy and individual spirit that would lead to a national park. Inspired by the mountains, the wildlife, and the challenge of life in the shadow of the Tetons, these people set the stage for what would follow. Ranchers, dudes, mountaineers, scientists, public servants all played a part.

EMORY J. ANDERSON PHOTO

James Manges

James Manges is representative of those early permanent residents. When he staked out his 160 acres just south of Jenny Lake in 1911, he was only the second person to homestead west of the Snake River in what is now Grand Teton National Park. When Manges left his cabin to go off on snowshoes and fish for cutthroat trout in the Snake River he would tack a handwritten sign on the front door: "Gone fishing. If I don't come back try to make a living off the place."

This concept, that the landscape is larger than any individual, and it cannot be owned by anyone, was the force behind the formation of Grand Teton National Park. James Manges, John D. Rockefeller, Jr., Margaret E. Murie, Horace Albright, Pierce Cunningham, and others recognized that this was a special place and needed to be set aside.

James Manges's cabin today

Prehistoric Times

While the landscape we know as Jackson Hole and the Tetons dates back millions of years, the first evidence of humans living in this region points to a time about 12,000 years ago. These people of the Paleoindian Period inhabited sites surrounding the valley, and, as the Jackson Hole glaciers melted, they walked over the mountain passes and up the river canyons to get here. This was during the period between the melting of the large glaciers that completely filled the north end of the valley and the melting of smaller glaciers back into the Teton canyons. During this several-thousand-year interval, plants reestablished themselves, and animals returned.

Stone points dating back 11,000 years have been found in the Snake River Canyon just south of the park, and an 8,000 year-old obsidian knife was uncovered near a lake in the northern park. Campsites in the northern part of the park are also dated to 8,000 years ago and before. Obsidian, a volcanic glass used for knives and arrow points, was quarried both at the north end of the Teton Range and at the south, near Teton Pass, by the early inhabitants. Pieces of it were traded among tribes, and some made it all the way to tribes in present-day Ohio and beyond. Altogether, the archaeological evidence points to a strong, permanent population in this area with extensive ties to other tribes.

For several thousand years these prehistoric American Indians lived here during the spring, summer, and fall months. They lived and traveled in family groups and despite their subsistence way of life were as intelligent and civilized as any humans today. They did not have horses until they were brought in by the Spanish explorers about 1700 A.D. Early Ameican Indians walked everywhere they went and used dogs for their pack animals. They traveled a seasonal circuit that took them to various sites at specific times of year for hunting, fishing, and gathering plants. We have to remember that their entire lives were lived outdoors and knowing the locations of plants and animals was as much a part of their existence as grocery stores are to us today—they didn't just wander in search of food.

These people also migrated in response to droughts and other natural events. When the Indians reached Jackson Hole, they collected plant foods such as Blue Camas bulbs, berries, sedges, bistort, and others. They also hunted and fished in the valley, leaving in the fall to follow their seasonal routes.

They dried some of the plants, and they probably roasted others in fire pits. Although there are no roasting pits remaining here from the earliest times, slightly later ones have been uncovered by park archaeologists, mostly in the northern parts of the park where food plants were most abundant. These pits were built and used during the Archaic Period, from about 7,000 years before present (ybp) to just about 1,500 ybp.

The timeless landscape of Jackson Hole

Colter Bay Visitor Center and Indian Arts Museum

For a more complete understanding of the American Indian culture and the people who had this land to themselves for thousands of years, a visit to Colter Bay will enlighten visitors of all ages. The museum is home to the David T. Vernon Collection of Native American Arts, donated to the National Park Service by Laurance S. Rockefeller.

Cree Chippewa pouch, circa 1880

7

American Indians

American Indians have lived here continuously for at least the past 11,000 years, and their people, customs, and culture are still a vibrant part of the region today. Although that long span of time has been divided up into periods according to archaeological evidence, the people evolved in one constant, dynamic mix of tribes and bands. From those first prehistoric people to today's Shoshone, Bannock, and other tribes, all share a long and complex history. In their travels around the region, the prehistoric tribes of the Paleoindian Period came into contact with other tribes. Tools, adaptations, and ideas were naturally shared when they met, and over thousands of years their cultures evolved and blossomed into the modern tribes—Shoshone, Crow, and others—that first had contact with Europeans and Euroamericans.

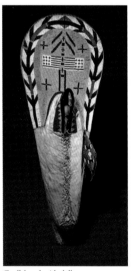

As the tribes evolved and their cultures changed with the arrival of European influences, especially the horse, their relationship to Jackson Hole changed. They were still nomadic, and their culture revolved around hunting, but now they could easily travel to find the resources they needed. Even more important, their cultures were undergoing radical changes with the arrival of Europeans, new weapons, and rapidly diminishing resources. The first Euroamerican explorers found trails through the valley and hunting and foraging parties, but no permanent residents in the Euroamerican sense of dwellings and agriculture. These explorers saw the valley as basically a wild and, in their view, an "unclaimed" place. The resulting wars, conflict with fur trappers, and eventual relocation to reservations created profound cultural changes in the American Indian tribes.

Cradleboard with doll

Another factor that may have limited the use of Jackson Hole was a period of unstable climate, known as the Little Ice Age, with times of extreme cold. This occurred from about 1400 A.D. to about 1850 A.D., and is the period when the modern-day glaciers formed in the Tetons.

The following tribes, plus the Northern Cheyenne, Northern Arapahoe and others, have long and historic ties to this valley and the Teton Range. The American Indian tribes received names from the European explorers, and over time those names have replaced the various tribes' own names.

"It was their way to pass through a country without disturbing anything, like the fish in the water and the birds that fly through the air." Laine Thom, Shoshone-Bannock, 2006

Shoshone

The tribe most closely associated with Jackson Hole and the Tetons, the Shoshone (known to early Euroamericans as the Snake Indians), ranged from the Northern Plains to the Southwest U.S. The Shoshone are relatives of the Comanche, and it was through them that the Shoshone acquired horses and thus the ability to expand their hunting strategies. All the Shoshone bands spoke the same language and considered themselves one large tribe, but they naturally fell into certain divisions by geography. The Eastern Shoshone, to the east of the Continental Divide, and the Shoshone-Bannock, to the west of the Tetons, probably had the closest ties to this valley. The Shoshone also divided themselves into smaller bands based on their preferred game. There were the Sheep Eaters (Tukudika), the Buffalo Eaters (Kucundicka), and so on.

The Shoshone continue to have close spiritual ties to the Tetons.

The Sheep Eaters (Tukudika) were a small band of Shoshone that preferred the high country in and around the Yellowstone area. They never acquired horses, but lived well in the mountains using dogs for pack animals. When Yellowstone was established as a national park the Sheep Eaters were forced to join other Shoshone on the Wind River Reservation east of Jackson Hole.

Chief Washakie was born in 1798, among the Flathead Indians of Montana and eventually became the last war chief for the Eastern Band of Shoshone. Washakie was an outstanding warrior, statesman, peacemaker, and interpreter. As his tribe underwent decades of change and was threatened by the steady advance of Euroamerican civilization, Washakie was able to negotiate a permanent home for his people. Although forced onto a reservation, Washakie had the skill and prestige to get the land that he and his people wanted, the Wind River country.

"I am laughing because I am happy. Because my heart is good. As I said two days ago, I like the country you mentioned, then, for us, the Wind River valley."

Washakie

Bannock

Relatives of the Northern Paiutes, the Bannock were powerful warriors when necessary and allied with the Shoshone at times of war. Eventually their fates merged when both tribes were given land on the Fort Hall Reservation in Idaho. They were essentially the same people, with the same culture and language, and today there are many Shoshone-Bannock people living in this area.

Blackfoot

The Blackfoot descended from the eastern Algonquian tribes and occupied the eastern base of the Rockies from Canada through Montana. The Blackfoot people were traditional enemies of the Shoshone and Nez Perce Indians and only ventured into the Teton area when hunting or at war. They were involved near the Tetons in 1839, in a fight with mountain man Joe Meek. Respected by their friends and feared by their enemies, the powerful Blackfoot had lost many of their people by the late 1800s, when smallpox and a lack of buffalo ended their reign. However, their strong culture and language have survived, and about 14,000 members of the Blackfoot Nation still live throughout the West.

Chief Taghee of the Bannock tribe was a contemporary and friend of Chief Washakie of the Shoshone. Taghee was known for being a powerful chief who negotiated his tribe's move to the reservation at Fort Hall, Idaho. The Bannock had been nomadic people, and Taghee insisted on retaining traditional hunting and foraging rights outside the reservation.

"I want the right to camp and dig roots on Canyon prairie when coming to Boise City to trade … I will go from here to buffalo country, where I will meet with all my tribe, and will tell them of this talk and of the arrangements we may make."

Gros Ventre

Also of the northern plains, the Gros Ventre tribe ventured south into Wyoming on occasion while on their way to visit their kinsmen, the Arapaho. Like the Blackfoot, they were determined enemies of the fur trappers. The Gros Ventre were involved in a clash with fur trappers just over the Tetons in Idaho and escaped through Jackson Hole. Gros Ventre was a name given by the early French trappers, but they called themselves A'aninin—White Clay People. The mountains and river to the east of Jackson Hole bear their name.

Crow

The Crow got their name from the Euroamericans' misinterpretation of their Indian name, Apsaalooke, which means "children of the large-beaked bird." That was interpreted as "Crow." Like most American Indian tribes, the Crow had their "home" grounds, but they were nomadic and followed the game as needed. They were as likely to be found west of the Tetons as east and used the mountains as a landmark to find the trails through Jackson Hole.

Many visitors to Grand Teton National Park mistakenly think of the American Indian tribes as a thing of the past. While the colorful, free-roaming culture of the 1700s and 1800s is gone, the tribes and their influence on the West still live on. Just as descendents of fur trappers and homesteaders live and work in this region, descendents of Indian statesmen, warriors, and families also live here.

View of Teton Range from Togwotee Pass

11

Trappers, Explorers, and Surveyors

Soon after the United States purchased the Louisiana Territory from France in 1803, President Thomas Jefferson sent the Lewis and Clark Expedition to explore the land and help establish a claim reaching all the way to the Pacific Ocean. The purchased territory only went as far west as the Continental Divide, so it barely missed Jackson Hole and the Tetons, but it included most of what is now Wyoming, much of Montana, and most of Yellowstone. A few French and British fur trappers were already scattered throughout the land.

The return of Lewis and Clark with a glowing report on the richness of the land and the friendliness of the Indians launched more trips, this time by men intent on trapping beaver. The latest fashion in Europe and the eastern U.S. had put men's stovepipe top hats in style, and the best fur available was beaver. Lewis and Clark reported great numbers of beaver at the headwaters of the Missouri.

John Colter

One young volunteer on the Lewis and Clark expedition was a man named John Colter. He didn't return to civilization with the expedition, but remained in the West hoping to benefit from his knowledge of the land. In 1807, he set out from a fort owned by trader Manuel Lisa and headed south toward Crow Indian country. He stumbled upon what was to become Yellowstone and all of its thermal wonders and may have wandered through Jackson Hole. As with many events of that era, there is no proof one way or the other. For many years John Colter was credited as the first white man to

Snake River and view north to Tetons as seen by trappers.

enter Jackson Hole, even though he himself had never claimed that distinction. The arguments against his visit are persuasive, and today most historians doubt that Colter ever visited Jackson Hole.

> *"Mountains piled on Mountains and capped with three spiral peaks which pierce the cloud. These peaks bear the name of Tetons or Teats—the Snake Indians call them the hoary headed Fathers."*
> **Osborne Russell, June 24, 1835**

For the next few years only a handful of fur trappers visited the valley, and in the winter of 1811-12, four of them stayed the winter and trapped. They were part of the John Jacob Astor party headed for Oregon. The War of 1812 interrupted the American fur trade for a few years, but by the mid-1820s, it was back in full swing. During this period all the legendary mountain men passed through Jackson Hole or stayed to trap beaver here including Jedediah Smith, Jim Bridger, Tom Fitzpatrick, and William Sublette. One of these trappers, David E. Jackson, was given the honor of having his favorite valley named for him—Jackson's Hole. In those days a valley surrounded by mountains was referred to as a "hole."

Mountain man Jim Bridger first passed by the Tetons in 1825, and he returned to Jackson Hole many times while trapping beaver and exploring the region. Although he was unschooled and signed his name with an 'X', Bridger was widely known as the foremost explorer of the Rockies. Jim Bridger passed on his extensive knowledge of the geography to scientific explorers such as Raynolds and Hayden. Bridger was married to the daughter of Chief Washakie of the Shoshones, and through their long friendship the two men learned much about each other's culture.

This was not the richest trapping area, but there were plenty of beaver for a

handful of trappers to work the streams and ponds below the Tetons. More important, this valley was a crossroads of many trails, all tied to the greatest landmark for miles around—Les Trois Tetons. Everyone working in the fur trade knew exactly where they were as soon as they saw the three highest peaks of the Tetons looming above the horizon. Named by lonely French trappers, les Trois Tetons (the Three Breasts) were also called the Pilot Knobs. Of course, the American Indians knew them by other names, such as "the Hoary Headed Fathers" or "the Ghost Robbers." For the Indians, the peaks were not just landmarks, but were a place of spiritual connection.

The decade from 1830 to 1840 saw the slow demise of the fur trade and the end of one of the country's most colorful ways of life. In 1835, Jackson Hole was visited by Osborne Russell, one of the few trappers to document a mountain man's life in a diary. Osborne's book *Journal of a Trapper* was published after his death. The last rendezvous was held in 1840 near the Green River, and the mountain men scattered to find other lives. A few continued to hunt and trap, and some of them signed up to lead pioneers westward.

Davey Jackson

Born in Virginia in 1788, David E. Jackson was already thirty-three years old when he joined a trading company and headed up the Missouri to begin his career as a fur trapper. When attacked by Arikara Indians after their horses, Jackson escaped with William Sublette. According to a friend, *"Sublette and Jackson after fighting bravely around the animals, until all were either killed or dispersed, fought their way through the crowded ranks of Indians, leaped into the river, and under a hail storm of arrows and balls, swam to the boats."*

Jackson formed a trapping company with Sublette and Jedediah Smith and spent most of his active fur trapping days in Jackson Hole, named for him by Sublette in 1829. In the spring of 1830, Jackson left his favorite valley for the last time. He died in Paris Tennessee in 1837. History did not leave much evidence of this quiet man's character, but as one historian noted, " ... *the lake and valley among the Tetons that bear his name are monuments sublime and enduring enough for any man."*

Beaver country

Scientific Expeditions

One thing that all the mountain men had going for them after the fur trade collapsed was an intimate knowledge of the Rocky Mountains. They had explored every valley and stream, discovered all the mountain passes, and knew where all the dangers were. A few trappers made use of their knowledge by guiding groups of settlers through the Rockies or scouting for the U.S. Army. In 1860, their skills were first put to use in opening up the Jackson Hole area.

That year, Captain William Raynolds was sent to survey the possibility of building a railroad through the area surrounding Yellowstone to assess the existing wagon roads and trails and to make a general survey of Indian numbers, natural resources, and climate. All this was in anticipation of the U.S. Army's role in the country's westward expansion. Raynolds' guide was Jim Bridger, the legendary mountain man known for his unfailing sense of direction. However, Bridger hadn't been in the area for a number of years and got disoriented. When spring snows forced the party to detour through Jackson Hole, he took Raynolds the full length of the valley and left via Teton Pass. This expedition was the first of its kind here,

Osborne Russell
Surprisingly, a number of the rough and wild fur trappers were well-educated young men who left their eastern farms searching for a new way of life. Osborne Russell was one of those, and he kept a diary of his adventurous life in the mountains. Russell often trapped for beaver in Jackson Hole, recalling in his journal that he spent a miserable July 4th, 1885, on the banks of the Snake River after capsizing while trying to cross:
"I now began to reflect on the miserable condition of myself and those around me, without clothing or provisions or fire arms and drenched to the skin with the rain ... a group of human beings crouched round a fire which the rain was fast diminishing meditating on their deplorable conditions ... ."

In 1876, Lieutenant Gustavus Doane led a small survey party of soldiers into Jackson Hole. The winter trip produced no scientific information, and in fact became a disaster with Doane and his men forced to eat one of their horses and a river otter to survive. Despite all the hardships, Doane's report was full of enthusiasm for the beautiful Teton country, the first hint that the scenery itself was a resource to be saved:

"There are no foothills to the Tetons. They rise suddenly in rugged majesty from the rock strewn plain. Masses of heavy forest appear on the glacial debris and in parks behind the curves of the lower slopes, but the general field of vision is glittering glaciated rock. The soft light floods the great expanse of the valley, the winding silvery river and the resplendent deeply carved mountain walls."

as it included scientists to collect and describe what they saw. In Raynolds' party was a young man named Ferdinand V. Hayden, a physician with a strong interest in geology and exploration.

Two other military surveys passed through the valley, including a disastrous one led by Lieutenant Gustavus Doane in the winter of 1876. This ended up becoming a survival trip, with no useful information collected, but Doane was awed by the sheer beauty of the Tetons.

By this time, civilian expeditions were replacing military ones. The U.S. Geological Survey of the Territories was formed, and in 1871, Congress budgeted $40,000 to survey the land that would become Yellowstone and its surrounding lands. The party was to be led by Ferdinand V. Hayden, the veteran of Raynolds' 1860 expedition through Jackson Hole. Hayden took along photographer William H. Jackson and artist Thomas Moran, and it was their work that helped persuade Congress to create Yellowstone National Park the following year.

Hayden was popular with congressmen as well as with industry, and he was able to put together well-financed expeditions to survey the West for its resources. In 1872, he led a sixty-one-man party back to Yellowstone, but this time he sent half the men under the leadership of James Stevenson to explore the Snake River country and the Tetons. They camped on the west side of the Tetons, mapped them from that side, then continued on up to Yellowstone. Among other guests, Stevenson took along the new superintendent of Yellowstone, Nathaniel Langford, and photographer William H. Jackson. Both these men would play important roles in the history of this area.

Another vital member of the party was their guide, a red-bearded former mountain man and fur trapper named Richard "Beaver Dick" Leigh. Born in England, he had fought in the war with Mexico and then

"rane with heavy thunder and lightning every 2 hours thrue the night betwixt storms the moone wold shine out clere. The heavey clouds commenced to rase to the top of mount moran and the Big Teton. at noone every cloud was gone."
Richard Leigh

found a life in the Rockies as a
hunter and trapper. Leigh was
married to a Shoshone woman and
living in a tipi when Stevenson
hired him. Leigh had explored the
whole west side of the mountains
as well as Jackson Hole to the east.

*"The Tetons have loomed up grandly
against the sky. From this point it is
perhaps the finest pictorial range in the
United States or even N. America."*
Thomas Moran

Guide Richard Leigh and his wife Jenny received the timeless honor of
having two lakes named for them by the 1872 Hayden Survey: Jenny Lake
and Leigh Lake. Little did they know that these two glacial lakes would be
enjoyed one hundred years later by millions of Teton visitors. Sadly, just four
years after guiding the expedition, Jenny, Richard, and their children con-
tracted smallpox. Jenny and the children died, but Richard recovered and
lived in Idaho until 1899.

William H. Jackson was a pioneer in the new art of photography, working with heavy glass plates and a portable
darkroom setup that he packed around on mules. Jackson
scrambled up onto Table Mountain with its spectacular,
panoramic views of the Tetons and captured the first photographs of these mountains. These would be the first
images of the Tetons ever to reach the outside world.

HARRISON R. CRANDALL PHOTO

W.H. Jackson, ca. 1930

Meanwhile, Stevenson and Langford were off on their
own adventure. On July 29, 1872, the two men attempted
to climb the Grand Teton, leaving the rest of the climbing party at one
point and pushing on for the top. Their claim to have reached the summit
ignited a controversy a few years later when William Owen and his party
successfully climbed the peak and found no evidence of any previous ascent.

*W.H. Jackson took this photo of the U.S. Geological Survey in camp in 1870. Seated in the center of the
back row is F.V. Hayden, U.S. geologist in charge. Jackson is standing with hat on far right.*

NPS PHOTO

Cowboying at the Triangle X Ranch

Homesteaders and Ranchers

The Homestead Act of 1862 opened large areas of public land in the West for anyone to claim a piece of land. One hundred sixty acres could be had for a $15 fee and a bit of paperwork. The only catch was that homesteaders had to live on and work the land for five years before they could get title to it.

Jackson Hole was known by many of the ranchers and farmers in surrounding areas, but it wasn't appealing to them. The valley was at a high altitude, it was isolated, and the cold climate prevented most kinds of agriculture. It would take a different type of person to survive in this valley. Even with all the problems, nearly 400 pieces of land were claimed within the present-day boundaries of Grand Teton National Park during the almost fifty-year period that Jackson Hole was open for homesteading.

In 1884, former mountain men John Holland and John Carnes, along with Carne's wife, hauled their farm equipment and supplies on mules into Jackson Hole. They entered the valley from the east on a trail from the Green River, up and over the divide and down the Gros Ventre River, following the same path they had used previously when they trapped beaver in the valley. They were the first to homestead in Jackson Hole.

More homesteaders followed, although there was definitely no "land rush" as in other parts of the country. By 1888, only twenty-three hardy individuals lived here. These first residents claimed land on the valley floor where wild grass grew so they would have that to feed their livestock while they cleared, plowed, and planted more acres. The best land was near Flat Creek, Spring

Gulch, Wilson, and the fields south of the town of Jackson. Homesteaders also selected land for its soil, water, protection from the elements, and proximity to other resources such as timber. As homesteaders spread north through the valley, they chose land that would support agriculture.

> "Hell, I hooked up the team on the plow and tried to make a furrow. It was so rocky I couldn't even get the plow into the ground. I just looked around and I couldn't see a place that wasn't rocky, so I loaded up the plow and came home."
>
> **Si Ferrin**, 1900

Jackson Hole seemed to attract more than its share of characters, and until the 1890s, it was largely a valley of bachelors. Perhaps it was the isolation, the atmosphere of being a unique place, even the rugged scenery that drew them here. Ex-soldiers and trappers, foreigners, more than a few outlaws, and people wanting to start over found their way over the mountains and into the picturesque valley.

In 1889, a group of Mormon families, driven from Utah by drought, arrived and claimed land. By 1890, sixty people lived in Jackson Hole. As a sense of community developed and dependable roads and trails were built, the valley attracted more and more families. Smaller communities sprang up where the land was good or where other resources attracted people. Eventually, homesteaders arrived who had no intention of committing themselves to the hard life of a Jackson Hole farmer—their interest lay in the scenery, the wildlife, and the mystique of the Tetons.

Menor's Ferry

Bill Menor's ferry carries a car across the river.

Other than land near Wilson at the foot of Teton Pass, only one homestead claim was made on the west side of the river during the 1890s. This was William D. Menor, who actually squatted on the land for twelve years before getting title to it. Bill Menor chose a short stretch of the Snake River where the meandering stream confined itself to one channel, with solid banks on both sides. He built a ferry, with a system of cables,

Bill Menor was known as a confirmed bachelor and a grouch, and for his profane language. He was also known to refuse his services to anyone he didn't want to ferry across the Snake River. To his friends and neighbors, however, he was fair and good.

But he was outdone by his brother Holiday Menor, who arrived in Jackson Hole thirteen years later and took up a homestead directly across the river from Bill's place. Holiday swore even more and had a worse temper than Bill. At one point they apparently had a brotherly spat and didn't speak to each other for two years. Both brothers eventually sold out and moved from the valley in the 1920s.

docks, and a wooden pontoon boat for crossing the river. For many years Menor's Ferry was the only place to cross the Snake in the heart of Jackson Hole, and it proved vital in the early years of life on the land that would become Grand Teton National Park.

Menor's Ferry was a seasonal operation, starting up when the spring floods were over and shutting down in fall when the water dropped too low. In 1907, the dam at the mouth of Jackson Lake collapsed, wiping out Menor's Ferry. It was rebuilt that summer.

Menor's Ferry, with its ferry crossing, store, and blacksmith shop, was the center of the Moose area. Other homesteaders, including Bill Menor's brother Holiday, settled directly across the river. The Dornan family's business, visible across the river from the ferry, is located on land homesteaded by Evelyn Dornan in 1922. Bill Menor sold out to Maude Noble in 1918, and then a steel bridge built at the site in 1927 made the ferry obsolete. Today, the buildings are preserved and open to the public. A replica of the ferry operates during the summer if water conditions permit.

> *"The last time I ever wash a diaper, I'm going to raise it on a flagpole and fly it like a flag until it turns to shreds."* Ida Chambers, Mormon Row mother of seven

Mormon Row

The first homesteaders to settle in the area known as Mormon Row reached their land via Menor's Ferry, traveling up the west side of the valley from Teton Pass and crossing at Moose in 1896. They staked claims, built homes, farmed, and raised cattle. After President Theodore Roosevelt opened up land northeast of Blacktail Butte in 1908, others settled on the area of deep topsoil just north of the earlier farmers, creating a line of houses, barns, and cabins. Since most of these families were Mormon, the area became known as Mormon Row. The names of this area's residents are synonymous with Jackson Hole's early days: May, Budge, Moulton, Chambers, and others. Large families and hard work were the way of life.

Mormon Row is situated on the end of a large alluvial fan of deep soil that spreads east from Ditch Creek. The soil is rich, but water is over one hundred feet down, and the early wells had to be dug by hand. The farmers made do with water from Ditch Creek and dry farmed oats and wheat. Eventually, water was brought by irrigation ditches all the way

from the Gros Ventre River. Most of the farmers raised hay and cattle, along with produce, eggs, and milk. During the heyday of the dude ranches across the Snake River, the farms along Mormon Row provided much of the fresh food they needed.

Today, a number of the original buildings still stand along the same dirt road running between Antelope Flats Road and the Kelly road. The northern-most farm buildings, including the pink farmhouse, are on land homesteaded by John A. Moulton in 1916. The classic Moulton barns, photographed for more years than they served as barns, are on the homesteads of T.A. and John Moulton. Both of these properties were later sold to the National Park Service. Most of the remaining old buildings belonged to Andrew Chambers. A few hardy people tried their luck at farming north of Mormon Row in the cobble and sagebrush of Antelope Flats. Joe Pfeiffer managed to eke out a living until he died, and his rustic homestead later burned in a 1994 sagebrush wildfire.

Cottonwood Creek

Water was key to farming in the dry climate of Jackson Hole, so homestead-ers looked for sites with good, year-round streams. One of these places, which didn't have much soil but had incredible views of the Tetons, was the land along Cottonwood Creek. This stream begins at the outlet of Jenny Lake and winds its way about seven miles to join the Snake River just above Moose.

First to settle in this area was James "Uncle Jim" Manges, a young farmer on his way to Montana in 1910. Manges liked the valley, and spent a year tromping around and looking at available land. All the prime farmland in the valley was already claimed, so Manges decided that if he couldn't have good soil, he'd have a good view and plenty of wildlife to hunt. He chose his 160 acres along Cottonwood Creek. After five hard years of "proving up" he earned his land, but it was always a struggle to get by. As a small example of the kind of life he lived, he had chickens but never ate a fresh egg—he pickled the extra summer's eggs for winter, and since he always ate the oldest eggs first, he never caught up. He did the same with his hand-churned butter, eating the old-est, rancid butter first. In 1917, he found a new source of income, one that would change his life and become the foundation of a new kind of busi-ness in Jackson Hole—he rented one of his cabins to a woman from the East. Eventually Manges would make his living renting cabins to "dudes" each summer.

HARRISON R. CRANDALL PHOTO

Geraldine Lucas

Just north of Jim Manges's place was the home-stead of schoolteacher Geraldine Lucas. She took over a homestead in 1913, with plans to build a

Lucas/Fabian place

home for her retirement. She cultivated land and made improvements, and by 1922, the property was hers. Just two years later she persuaded Paul Petzoldt, a young mountain climber, to take her up the Grand Teton. At the time she was fifty-nine and not in climbing condition, but Petzoldt managed to help her to the summit. Geraldine was the second woman to climb the Grand. Before the climb she told Petzoldt that she not only wanted to climb the Grand because she loved it, but to prove herself to the residents. She told Petzoldt, "I've heard talk around town that it's no place for a woman and that women should not be allowed up there. People just don't understand women like myself."

Geraldine Lucas loved the isolation and the beauty of her homestead along Cottonwood Creek. When approached by John D. Rockefeller Jr.'s Snake River Land Company (formed to buy up private land near the Tetons) to sell her ranch she reportedly said, "You stack up those silver dollars as high as the Grand Teton, and I might talk to you."

After her death, her property was purchased by Harold Fabian for the Rockefellers and was donated to the park. Her home is still standing and is known as the Geraldine Lucas cabin.

Lupine Meadows and Jenny Lake

Homesteaders in Jackson Hole not only had a difficult time making a living in this alpine valley, but they had to keep up to date on the homesteading rules, which were constantly changing. Almost all public land in the country

27

was opened for settlement by the Homestead Act of 1862, but then the Forest Reserve of 1891 withdrew the Yellowstone Timber Reserve, a large area that included the northern end of this valley. The 1897 Teton Forest Reserve then withdrew most of the land in Jackson Hole, but the 1908 creation of the Teton National Forest reopened the valley while protecting the mountains and forests. In 1916, the Wyoming state government tried to have Jenny Lake and Leigh Lake withdrawn so their water could be used for irrigation downstream. This wasn't settled until 1922, when the state lost its bid and the land around Jenny Lake was reopened for homesteading. Beginning in 1927, several congressional acts began to close off homesteading, and by 1930, it was over.

> *"We have to finish the house. Sheds must be built for the cattle before winter comes. I have to make some corrals; and before hay is ready to cut we have to get a mowing machine and a rake into the country. Got to go to St. Anthony for those things; it'll take a week for that trip. Then we have to put up hay—should have a hundred tons, but we won't. We'll do the best we can, but the summer's short."*
>
> Jack Shive, 1897

In the period between 1922 and 1927, there was a mini land rush for homesteads around Jenny and Leigh Lakes, land which had been off limits for five years. Although the law stipulated that the land was to be used for agricultural purposes and most settlers were at least part-time farmers or ranchers, a few creative individuals managed to find ways around the law.

In 1922, the Danny Ranch was started near the east shore of Jenny Lake—it would later become the present-day Jenny Lake Lodge. A man named Ed "Roan Horse" Smith took over an abandoned homestead of 160 acres in Lupine Meadows. Homer Richards filed for 160 acres just southeast of Jenny Lake. He grazed cattle on 18 acres and built a gas station and rental cabins on the rest. Harrison Crandall, the noted Teton photographer, claimed 120 acres just north of the present-day Jenny Lake Lodge. Crandall grew 20 acres

Harrison Crandall at his studio, 1920s

of brome grass and grazed 40 horses to comply with the law while he built a log studio and started his photography business. And out in the meadow where the Cathedral Group Turnout presently sits, Albert Gabbey made two claims for raising livestock and opened the Square G Guest Ranch.

Ranching

Cunningham Cabin

Of course, not all of the homesteaders took small claims just as places to live or for land speculation. Cattle ranching was still the largest and most respected industry of the day, and there were a few areas within the present-day park boundaries that offered homesteaders a decent chance at success. Most of the better land for growing hay and raising cattle was in the south end of the valley, but a few early settlers found productive land in the north. Others, like Stephen Leek, established a ranch on land in the southern part of the valley and either claimed or squatted on land near the Tetons for other pursuits. Leek built a hunting lodge on the shores of Leigh Lake and later established a much larger camp on the eastern shore of Jackson Lake.

Pierce Cunningham arrived in 1885, and lived for a few years as a trapper. In 1888, he homesteaded just south of Spread Creek, built a cabin, and began a long and successful career as a cattle rancher in Jackson Hole. His original cabin still stands on the old homestead in Grand Teton National Park. Cunningham supported the preservation of the valley by encouraging his fellow ranchers to consider selling out to the National Park Service.

Si Ferrin moved to Jackson Hole around 1900, hoping to claim a homestead along the Buffalo River near Moran. The land was closed for settling while the state and federal governments negotiated over rights, so Ferrin farmed and worked around the valley. In 1908, the land re-opened and Ferrin made his claim. He pros-

The Elk Ranch

pered and bought up other property nearby, including the old Elk Ranch. Eventually Si Ferrin built the Elk Ranch into the largest cattle operation in the valley. By 1928, when he and his sons sold their property to the Rockefeller family interests, they had over 3,600 acres. The Elk Ranch can still be seen just south of Moran Junction, in the broad fields and meadows to the east of the highway.

NPS PHOTO

Bill Menor's ferry in operation

Historic Communities

As the valley grew from its first homesteaders in 1884, small communities sprang up where settlers concentrated around good land, water, or near friends or family members. Some of those early communities survived to the present, but others disappeared over the years. Many were little more than a post office that anchored an area of settlement.

Elk, Wyoming was just such an arrangement. One of the earliest post offices in the valley, it moved from ranch to ranch in the area of Spread Creek and the Elk Ranch, finally settling on the Moosehead Ranch. At times, a store accompanied the post office.

The community of Moose got its start when Bill Menor homesteaded in 1894 and built his ferry, store, and blacksmith shop, although it was known as Menor's Ferry until 1929. The area had a church, a school, a store, and a number of inhabitants. Today, Bill Menor's buildings still sit on the banks of the Snake River. Dornan's, settled in 1922, thrives across the river. The Maude Noble cabin and other historical buildings still dot the landscape.

Kelly sits right on the eastern edge of the park, along the Gros Ventre River. It began with a few homesteads, then a bridge was built over the river and the area was known as "the Bridge." A school was built in 1909, followed by a flour mill, a sawmill, and more homes. By 1921, Kelly was competing with the town of Jackson as the county seat, and by 1926, it had stores, a hotel, post office, churches, a school, telephone service, and a livery stable. In May 1927, the natural dam, which had formed upstream when the north side of Sheep Mountain slid into the river, broke and released a torrent of water. The flood wiped out Kelly, killing six people and leaving only the church, rectory, and school buildings. Today, Kelly is a residential area with a few buildings that date back to the years just after the flood. In 1999, a safe from the Kneedy residence was discovered two miles downstream, half buried in the banks of the Gros Ventre River.

Other small community centers that disappeared include Grovont (their phonetic spelling) with a post office, school, and church on Mormon Row east of Blacktail Butte; Antler—a post office near Moran; and a fair-sized government town named Moran when the Jackson Lake Dam was under construction around 1910-11.

> *"The morning of May 18, 1927 was clear and warm. For about four days the snow had been melting rapidly and all streams had risen to considerable height. At about 10:30 the waters began rising at the estimated rate of one foot a minute and shortly afterward the bridge at Kelly went out.*
>
> *The crest of the flood as it burst upon the town was a terrifying sight, for it carried a twenty-five-feet high battering front of logs, trees, houses, and outbuildings.*
>
> *Every business house and residence was swept away and left not a trace of their former location. The church and schoolhouse, being on a higher elevation of land, escaped destruction.*
>
> *The battering wall of the flood hit the Gros Ventre River highway bridge half way from floor to top of steel, and the great spans rose up and dropped into the current. At times great logs leaped high in the air like barbed monsters of the sea."*
>
> — J.R. Jones, local homesteader

Gros Ventre Slide in 1927

Outlaws and Characters

Isolated, beautiful, and filled with out-of-the-way spots where a person could hide from civilization for years, Jackson Hole attracted more than its share of eccentric characters and people with uncertain pasts. The valley had a reputation for harboring wanted outlaws as long as they behaved themselves. Many of the residents of the valley had come here themselves to start over, some as wanted men, so they were more tolerant than in many western communities. Besides, it seemed in character with the unique landscape and harsh climate to have a handful of outlaws hanging out in the valley. When it came time for justice, the residents preferred to do it themselves.

JHHSM. 1918.0001.001

Teton Jackson

Teton Jackson probably used the valley for his horse stealing operations even before the first homesteaders arrived in 1884. He stole horses in Idaho and drove them to Jackson Hole and over to central Wyoming, where he sold them and stole some more horses. He drove those back to Jackson Hole and on to Idaho. Jackson was a family man and was well-liked in the valley, and he never stole from the locals.

Working from his little log cabin on Jackson Lake, Ed Trafton stole horses, robbed stage coaches in Yellowstone, and generally carried on a life of crime including stealing his father's life insurance money from his mother. He apparently met the writer Owen Wister, who frequented the valley in the early 1900s, and became the model for a villainous character in Wister's *The Virginian*. On one of his crime sprees from his remote cabin, Trafton reportedly went to Yellowstone one day and held up sixteen sightseeing coaches in a row.

In 1886, a fishing party discovered three bodies on the banks of the Snake River, just below what is now the Snake River Overlook along highway U.S. 89/191 north of Moose. The men were identified as three German gold prospectors who had been working the area. The fourth German, named Tonnar, was missing. A posse of local men eventually tracked him down over the mountains in Idaho, arrested him, and sent him to the county seat in the town of Evanston. As a gruesome touch, two men cut off the heads of the three bodies and prepared the skulls as evidence. But Tonnar pleaded self-defense and was let go. The upshot of this was to reinforce the locals' opinions that they should resort to their own form of justice when it was required. The place where the bodies were found on a gravel bar is still known as Deadman's Bar and is a popular boat launch for rafts and canoes.

In 1892, the philosophy of local justice met its end when two men, Spenser and Burnett, arrived with a herd of horses and made a deal with rancher Pierce Cunningham to use his original homestead cabin near Spread Creek. That winter two more men, claiming to be U.S. marshals, convinced a handful of local men to help them get Spenser and Burnett, whom they said were horse thieves. The posse crept up on the cabin and in the ensuing gunfight both Spenser and Burnett were killed. They were buried nearby. However, the men who had helped the marshals began to doubt their story, and soon no one would talk about the incident. It began to appear as if the two "lawmen" had duped the local men into helping them even the score on a grudge, or they were killers hired to find the two men and recapture the horses without involving the real law.

JHHSM_1958.0001.001

John Dudley Sargent

One of the more unusual characters who resided here was John Dudley Sargent, the illegitimate son of a wealthy eastern family. Although most characters who came here contributed to the growth or direction of the community, Sargent definitely did not. He was a "remittance man," given a stipend and sent west to avoid embarrassing the family. Sargent homesteaded on the eastern shore of Jackson Lake with his wife and five children and built a ten-room log cabin he named *Merymere*. He began offering room and board to travelers. A few years later, they were joined at *Merymere* by Robert Hamilton, a descendant of Alexander Hamilton. During a search for stray cattle one day, Hamilton drowned under suspicious circumstances, but Sargent wasn't charged. Sargent's wife then died of injuries (Sargent blamed them on a skiing accident) even after being discovered at *Merymere* and taken away for treatment. Sargent left the valley for a number of years, only to return to Jackson Lake with his mentally unstable new wife, whom he was being paid to care for. She was often seen sitting naked in a tree, playing her violin. She was finally taken away and Sargent took his own life in *Merymere*.

(overleaf) The meandering Snake River separated Jackson Hole communities.

The Second Wave

Following the initial homesteading and settling of the valley, a "second wave" of people found their way here, were impressed with the landscape, and either took up residence or bought property. Author and dude rancher Struthers Burt noted in 1927 that " … each summer more and more rich Easterners are buying places … ." It was difficult to make a living in the valley, and many of the original homestead properties were abandoned or sold and taken up by people whose livelihood didn't depend on the poor Teton topsoil. In many ways these people had a bigger impact on the present day park since their ownership of the land spanned the years Grand Teton National Park was being established. Some of the sites are still here.

Mardy Murie, 1927

Not all newcomers were wealthy. In 1927, biol-ogist Olaus Murie and his wife Margaret (Mardy) moved to the town of Jackson. Olaus studied the valley's elk and spent summers in wild country north of Jackson Lake. In 1945, he and Mardy and his brother Adolph and wife Louise bought the old STS dude ranch near Moose. This rustic old homestead became the unofficial center of conservation in the United States over the next fifty years as Olaus became a founding member of The Wilderness Society, Mardy wrote books and lobbied for conservation, and Adolph and Louise worked on his studies of wolves and grizzlies in Alaska. The property was eventually sold to the park by the Muries, and today the ranch is home to the Murie Center, a nonprofit conservation organization based on the Muries' philosophy of wilderness preservation.

Snowshoes

A few parcels of land were originally leased by the Forest Service before coming under National Park Service (NPS) control, and these continue to have a place in park history. In 1930, Ben Sheffield leased a summer home site overlooking Jackson Lake, and after his cabin burned he sold the lease to the wealthy Brinkerhoff family. They had a beautiful log home built, complete with furniture by Thomas Molesworth and the finest accessories from around the country. In 1955, they sold the property to the NPS, and today it is used to host people visiting on official park business.

Mardy and Olaus Murie House

Another site that evolved from an original homestead is the AMK Ranch, also on the shore of Jackson Lake. First owned by the eccentric John D. Sargent (see Outlaws and Characters above), the property was purchased by W. Lewis Johnson in 1926. Johnson was a retired Hoover Vacuum executive. He died a few years later, and in 1936, the property was purchased by the members of the Berol family, owners of the Eagle Pencil Company. They developed it into the luxurious but rustic AMK Ranch. In 1976, the ranch was sold to the National Park Service (NPS), and today it houses the cooperative NPS/University of Wyoming Research Center.

In 1944, William and Eileen Hunter bought the old Williams homestead on the eastern park border and built a small cattle ranch as their retirement project. The property was sold to the NPS in 1957, and some of the buildings still stand. The Hunter residence was relocated a few miles away to the site of the present-day Teton Science School.

Dozens of other home sites, ranches, and farms came and went over the years. Some of them still exist, but most have disappeared. Visitors with a strong interest in history can trace these places and their owners through time by reading some of the books available on the subject.

A valley of forests, meadows, and mountain views

Formation of Grand Teton National Park

If Jackson Hole had been more accessible during the early settling of the West, it might have filled with ranches and homes before the park could be set aside. As it was, the remoteness and difficulty of life for homesteaders kept the valley sparsely populated until a new national interest in conservation emerged in the early 1900s. Even so, the establishment of the park wasn't easy. Every act of legislation, every proposal for government control, and every attempt at preserving the land met with controversy. Looking back, it was a long fight that not only depended on a few determined individuals, but also on the effort to preserve other places and other resources. The park's formation can be attributed to six key events

> *"Of all places in the Rocky Mountains that I know, it is the most beautiful, and, as it lies too high for man to build and prosper in, its trees and waters should be kept from man's irresponsible destruction."*
>
> Owen Wister, 1892

Yellowstone National Park, 1872

With the establishment of Yellowstone, Congress opened a new era in legislation—laws to preserve and protect the West rather than to exploit it. The thermal wonders of the park caught the attention of the rest of the country, but its wildlife and other natural resources soon became just as intriguing to visitors. Early park managers realized that Yellowstone's wildlife didn't recognize boundaries, and that it would be necessary to protect some of the surrounding areas in order to preserve Yellowstone as it was. Many of the park elk, in fact, wintered in Jackson Hole where they were hunted.

Forest Reserve Act, 1891

Spurred by the disappearance of vast forests and the destruction of watersheds in the Midwest, a few concerned people convinced President Benjamin Harrison to save some of the land before it was all gone. With this far-reaching law it was possible for the president to set public land aside as a reserve without any specific function.

Teton National Forest, 1908

In 1905, Congress moved control of all the forest reserves from the Interior Department to the Department of Agriculture, and the Bureau of Forestry became the Forest Service. With that in place, President Roosevelt signed an executive order creating seven national forests out of the huge Yellowstone Forest Reserve. One of them was the Teton National Forest, a two million acre area that included the Tetons and most forests in Jackson Hole.

Grand Teton National Park, 1929

HARRISON R. CRANDALL PHOTO

Early park staff and visitors

Most Jackson Hole settlers and homesteaders opposed government control of the land, especially by any agency that kept the resources locked up. But when the winter range for the valley's famous elk herd needed protection, everyone supported the formation of the National Elk Refuge in 1912. Even though this marked a reversal in attitude, the valley's most powerful ranchers and businessmen continued to oppose a national park in their backyard.

Grand Teton was originally proposed as an extension of Yellowstone in the late 1800s, and for many years officials worked toward this plan. After decades of controversy and debate, Grand Teton National Park was finally established to include the Tetons and the land at their base. The creation of this small park of

39

only 96,000 acres ended the Yellowstone extension plan and left most of the valley as a forest reserve.

Still, some residents and a number of influential outsiders realized that commercial development would destroy the scenic nature of the valley and alter its western atmosphere. Grand Teton National Park was a compromise that still left much of the land unprotected.

Jackson Hole Monument, 1943

With an idea first put together at Maude Noble's log cabin in Moose in 1923, residents favoring protection of the valley launched the Jackson Hole Plan to buy up all the private land north of the town of Jackson (and in view of the Tetons). There was too much animosity toward the government for any agency to accomplish this, so the idea was to attract a wealthy individual to purchase these lands and protect them by donating them to the park.

Horace Albright

Horace Albright first visited the Tetons in 1916, while on an official tour of the Tetons. He was the 26-year-old assistant to the new Park Service director, and he added the valley to his list of places to protect. He wrote policy objectives for the new park system and, for many years, pushed to have the Tetons and Jackson Hole preserved as an extension of Yellowstone. Albright realized that the future of Jackson Hole lay not in cattle ranching but in tourism. He helped formulate the Jackson Hole Plan with valley residents, and he introduced John D. Rockefeller, Jr. to the Tetons. In 1919, he became superintendent of Yellowstone, and ten years later the director of the National Park Service. Throughout his entire public and private career, Horace Albright worked openly and behind the scenes to protect the Tetons.

John D. Rockefeller, Jr. entered the scene in the mid-1920s, and over the course of the next twenty or so years he would change the destiny of the valley. This phase of the park's history is a book in itself, but basically Rockefeller formed a private corporation called the Snake River Land Company and began buying up land in order to donate it to the government. His name and the purpose of the company were kept secret until 1930. Once the plan was out, a bitter and prolonged debate divided the valley. Many people thought the government already had enough land, while others saw a larger park as the only way to stop commercialism and preserve their rustic western way of life.

In 1943, President Franklin D. Roosevelt hoped to end the debate when he used his power of the 1906 Antiquities Act to issue a proclamation establishing the Jackson Hole National Monument. This monument of almost half a million acres included most of the valley east of the park, Jackson Lake, land taken from Teton National Forest, other public and state land, and almost 50,000 acres of private land including Rockefeller's 32,000 acres

Present-day Grand Teton National Park, 1950

Roosevelt's sudden establishment of the national monument in 1943 angered many in Jackson Hole. Armed ranchers protested by driving cattle into the protected lands, and the

> *"The Jackson Hole Plan is nothing more than an intelligent proposal to zone properly one of the most famous countries in the world, to prevent its selfish, or careless, despoliation, and to keep a proper balance between the various interests of the valley."* **Struthers Burt, Outdoor America, Nov.-Dec. 1944**

majority of the valley supported them. Except for the few people who favored preservation, the valley residents opposed the new status of their valley. They took the fight to the state and national government, and bills were quickly introduced to abolish the monument and repeal the Antiquities Act. Even the Forest Service objected to Roosevelt's proclamation.

An Armed Protest

Despite assurances by the National Park Service that traditional cattle grazing rights and access would be honored, local ranchers staged an armed ride in 1943, to protest the Jackson Hole Monument. Led by ranchers Peter Hansen and his son Clifford, the group enlisted Hollywood western actor Wallace Beery to ride with them. They rode unopposed, but earned a mention in *Time Magazine.* Clifford Hansen, who later became the governor and U.S. Senator, said, *"Thank God we lost that fight. I can just imagine what the valley would look like now without the Park to protect it."*

Clifford Hansen

Over the years from 1943 to 1949, the opposition slowly dwindled until only a handful of people were left. The National Park Service met with them and reached compromises on the major issues, including control of the elk herds, the loss of property tax revenues, and grazing rights. Finally, on September 14, 1950, President Harry Truman signed a bill formally changing the monument to the new 310,000-acre Grand Teton National Park of today.

CCC cleanup of the shores of Jackson Lake

Civilian Conservation Corps (CCC)

Soon after the original Grand Teton National Park was established, the Great Depression hit the country. One of the programs President Franklin D. Roosevelt launched as part of his New Deal to help the recovery was the Civilian Conservation Corps, known as the CCC. Up to 500 workers swarmed this new park for years, building trails, roads, bridges, and structures. One of their camps was next to Jenny Lake, and after the CCC left in 1942, the camp facilities were used by mountain climbers and guides.

The CCC also built new cabins and improved existing ones. They built the original superintendent's residence (still in use today) as well as other residences, garages, barns, and outbuildings.

The CCC built trails throughout the park, campgrounds and roadside turnouts, and established much of the park's early infrastructure such as water systems and roads. Visitors familiar with other national parks can often spot the enduring quality and style of those labor intensive CCC projects.

Trail built by CCC

One of the main CCC projects in Grand Teton was the cleanup of the shores of Jackson Lake. When the dam was built around 1911, the lake level rose 39 feet and flooded thousands of acres of trees. The CCC crews cleared 8,000 acres of shoreline of unsightly dead trees.

Jenny Lake Camp dedication

CCC Camp at Jenny Lake

Mountain Climbing

Although the entire Teton Range has a long and glorious history of mountain climbing, it was the Grand Teton that captured the attention of early mountaineers. Thought for many years to be unclimbable, the Grand thwarted a number of expeditions that attempted to reach its summit. Some of those attempts, a few of which were claimed to be successful, were not known about until decades or more after the event.

> *"The road came out of the forest into a meadow, swung over the lip of a canyon, and there, twenty-five miles across a valley, were the Tetons. I knew that the earth had done something about mountains here she hadn't done before. Because I came to climb them, they scared me a little, the steepness of them some, but mostly their perfection as mountains. Had I earned the right to approach these summits? That worry passed and was replaced by a feeling that whatever and wherever it was that I had been trying to get to, I had arrived."*
>
> Pete Sinclair, 1968

Prehistoric indigenous people and later, American Indians, no doubt explored the possibility of reaching the summit. They were here for thousands of years, revered the high peaks, and left evidence of their visitation. If one or more of them found their way to the top of the Grand, we will never know.

In the exploration of North America by Europeans and early Americans, only a few attempts were recorded or noted. The first seems to have been a man named Michaud LeClaire, who worked for the Hudson's Bay Company. He reportedly did not succeed in his 1843 effort. The second known attempt, almost thirty years later, became the most controversial.

Langford and Stevenson

During the 1872 Hayden Survey to explore and map the Teton and Yellowstone region, a party of fourteen made an attempt to reach the summit of the Grand. All but two turned back. James Stephenson, the survey's leader, and Nathaniel Langford, the superintendent of Yellowstone, claimed to have reached the top. Despite a detailed description of their climb published in *Scribner's Monthly* in 1873, the two men left no evidence of their success on the summit. This left the door open for future climbers to claim the first proven ascent. The controversy continues even today.

Charles Keiffer

> *"The Grand Teton is endlessly different, with its changing moods and attitudes, its eternal beauty. It is a friend—and it is always a privilege to climb it."*
>
> Glenn Exum

A second claimed ascent, again with no proof, came from three soldiers stationed in Yellowstone in 1893. Their claim did not come until 1899, when one of the men, Captain Charles Keiffer, wrote a letter in response to the first proven ascent (see below) the year before.

William O. Owen

In 1898, William O. "Billy" Owen, after a number of failed attempts, headed for the summit with five other climbers. Sponsored by the Rocky Mountain Club, they had two men drop out by the time they reached the Upper Saddle. The remaining four—Owen, Franklin Spaulding, Frank Petersen, and John Shive—were finally successful and returned two days later to repeat their feat and erect a stone cairn on the summit.

Owen immediately began a long, and apparently successful, publicity effort to establish his claim to owning the first ascent. He and Nathaniel Langford feuded publicly for years, and today others have picked up the case for both sides.

Eleanor Davis

The first woman to climb the Grand was a physical education teacher from Colorado, Eleanor Davis. She reached the summit in 1923 with legendary climber Albert Ellingwood.

Paul Petzoldt first climbed the Grand Teton in 1924. By the 1930s, he was guiding anyone who would hire him, and in 1931, he asked twenty-one-year-old trail crew member Glenn Exum to assist him in guiding a party of two Austrians up the Grand. Exum accidentally discovered a new route which now bears his name—the classic Exum Route.

In 1946, the two men formed the Petzoldt-Exum School of American Mountaineering, establishing the Tetons as the heart of American mountain guiding. Petzoldt had developed a system for climbers to communicate with each other and climb safely, and the two men stressed Petzoldt's system while guiding and teaching techniques. Under their leadership, the Exum Guide Service became one of the most well-known in the world.

By the 1960s, climbing in the Tetons had reached such a level of popularity that a second guide service opened: Jackson Hole Mountain Guides. Together, the two GTNP concessions have safely taught and guided thousands of visitors. Paul Petzoldt on why he climbed mountains: *"I can't explain this to other people. I love the physical exertion. I love the wind.*
I love the storms. I love the fresh air. I love the companionship in the outdoors. I love the reality. I love the change. I love the rejuvenating spirit. I love to feel oneness with nature. I'm hungry; I enjoy eating. I get thirsty; I enjoy the clear water. I enjoy being warm at night when it's cold outside. All those things are extremely enjoyable because, gosh, you're living them, your senses are really feeling. I can't explain it."

Major Peaks

Static Peak: *11,303. First ascent June 1934, by T.F. Murphy, Robert E. Brislawn. Named for its frequent lightning strikes.*

Buck Mountain:*11,938. First ascent August 21, 1898, by topographer T.M. Bannon and assistant George A. Buck via East Face. Bannon and Buck built a surveying cairn (stone marker) named "Buck Station"*

Veiled Peak:*11,330. First ascent September 18, 1932, by Phil Smith, Walcott Watson.*

Mt. Wister:*11,490. First ascent September 23, 1928, by Phil Smith, Oliver Zierlein. Named after Owen Wister, author of* The Virginian *and an early visitor to Jackson Hole.*

South Teton:*12,514. First ascent August 29, 1923, by Albert Ellingwood and Eleanor Davis (first woman to climb the Grand) via Northwest Couloir. Fifth highest peak in the range.*

Middle Teton:*12,804. First ascent August 29, 1923, by Albert Ellingwood. Named for its location among the other high peaks.*

Nez Perce:*11,901. First ascent July 5, 1930, by Fritiof Fryxell and Phil Smith via North Couloirs. Named for Nez Perce Indians who hunted in this region.*

Grand Teton:*13,770. First ascent August 11, 1898, by William Owen, Franklin Spaulding, Frank Petersen, and John Shive via Owen-Spalding Route. Renamed Mt. Hayden after Ferdinand V. Hayden but the name didn't stick.*

Mt. Owen:*12,928. First ascent July 16, 1930, by Robert Underhill, Kenneth Henderson, Fritiof Fryxell, Phil Smith via East Ridge. Named for William Owen, and last of the high peaks to be climbed.*

Teewinot Mountain:*12,325. First ascent August 14, 1929, by Fritiof Fryxell and Phil Smith via East Face. Name comes from Shoshone Indian word "Tee-Win-At" meaning "pinnacles."*

Mt. St. John:*11,430. First ascent August 20, 1929, by Fritiof Fryxell and Phil Smith. Named for Orestes H. St. John, geologist with the 1872 Hayden Expedition.*

Mt. Moran:*12,605. First ascent July 27, 1922, by LeGrand Haven Hardy, Ben C. Smith, and Bennet McNulty via Skillet Glacier. Named for landscape artist Thomas Moran.*

"I think we can beat Mount Owen this summer by head-work and brute strength. I'm in nearly perfect condition from logging and I'm going to keep that way. Women, whiskey, and cigarettes nearly ruined last season for me but I'm doing better and I expect to give Owen every ounce next July or August. We will cut or get around that terrific north snowfield if it kills us—are you game as ever?"

Phil Smith, letter to Fritiof Fryxell, 1929

(overleaf) The old Bar BC dude ranch

Dudes living the cowboy life

Dude Ranches

NPS PHOTO

Early dudes reach the park via airplane

It turned out that the sparse, glacially scoured land at the foot of the Tetons, despite being free, made for a tough life for homesteaders. Combined with long, severe winters, the land's unfertile soil forced many small ranchers and farmers into other lines of work to support their land claims. Some worked seasonally at timbering or building. A few of the ranchers began to take "boarders" during the summer months, and when they realized there was more money in "dudes" than in cattle, they gradually converted to dude wrangling. A dude was any outsider who paid for lodging, meals, horseback riding, and guiding services, and it was not a derogatory term.

Some of the best-known dude ranches were working cattle ranches that took in paying guests who wanted a taste of cowboy life. Others were operated as "guest ranches" and had no livestock besides horses. The early ranchers were reluctant to admit they were raising "dudes," but over time it became a very respectable business. The official definition eventually described those working ranches, or former working ranches, that took in paying guests and treated them to a taste of life in the old West.

The land at the foot of the Tetons, gifted with incredible scenery, wildlife, and a rustic, western atmosphere, became the perfect setting for dude ranches. These businesses were among the first to see the benefits of land preservation, and their owners were among the most vocal in saving the character, views, and uniqueness of Jackson Hole. Many former "dudes," through their early experiences in the Tetons, later moved here and became strong supporters of preservation.

The JY Ranch

Motoring across Phelps Lake

Located at the southern end of Phelps Lake, the JY is considered the first bona fide dude ranch in the valley. Other ranches no doubt took in guests, but this was the first operation built strictly for dudes. Louis Joy established it in 1907, and Struthers Burt joined him the next year. The land was worthless for farming and was obviously intended for dudes from the beginning. By 1927, the JY was the largest dude ranch in the valley, with thirty-eight buildings and a full array of western activities. In 1932, as land was being sold to the Rockefeller's Snake River Land Company for inclusion in an expanded GTNP, this ranch eventually came into the hands of John D. Rockefeller, Jr. and his family.

No single person was more vital to the preservation of this valley than John D. Rockefeller, Jr. Alarmed by commercial development at the foot of the mountains during a visit to the Tetons in 1926, he decided the only course of action was to buy all the land. Working patiently for two decades, Rockefeller funded the purchase of 35,000 acres of land. He donated the land to the park for its expansion in 1950. John D. Rockefeller, Jr. remained involved in the protection of Jackson Hole all of his life, and this tradition continued with his heirs. In 2001, his son Laurance S. Rockefeller gifted the family's last remaining property within the park, the magnificent JY Ranch, to the National Park Service as the "LSR Preserve." The property officially changed hands in 2006.

The Bar BC

The Bar BC

By 1911, Struthers Burt and Louis Joy had a falling out over the operation of the JY, and Burt went off on his own. Princeton educated and an aspiring author who needed a livelihood until his writing career took off, Burt joined up with a physician, Horace Carncross, to establish the Bar BC Ranch along the Snake River a few miles north of Moose. The men claimed adjoining homestead tracts and went to work. Their intention was to start with dudes and then revert to a working cattle ranch.

During the late 1920s, the Bar BC was one of the best-known dude ranches in the West and the center of dude social life. It combined a colorful western atmosphere with the rustic

> *"The dude wrangler is a ranch owner, a cowman, a horseman, a guide, a wholesale chambermaid, a cook, and a storekeeper rolled into one."*
> **Struthers Burt, 1934**

elegance of eastern society. This went on for a decade until events in the valley began to change life on the Bar BC. Carncross died in 1928, and then others associated with the running of the ranch died or moved on. Although Burt worked hard at convincing other ranchers to sell their property to the government as part of the proposed Grand Teton National Park, he was surprised to find that his own ranch was marked for purchase. He and Crancross's only heir, Irving Corse, eventually sold out but retained a lifetime lease.

Burt became a popular writer of his day, and his 1934 book *Diary of a Dude Wrangler* is a collector's item. The Bar BC continued to operate until 1986, but never quite regained the status it had during the heyday of dude ranching.

The White Grass

The White Grass before restoration.

In 1913, Harold Hammond took a claim on 160 acres at the base of Buck Mountain, and two years later his business partner, George Tucker Bispham, took 160 adjacent acres. With their lack of capital for improvements, Hammond had to work elsewhere, and he hired on at the Bar BC. Apparently the dude business made sense, and he and Bispham tried to combine farming and dude wrangling on their White Grass Ranch. They were unsuccessful, and in 1924, they sold out to the Bar BC. Under that successful ranch's supervision, the White Grass became a popular place. It was also a silver fox farm as well as a dude ranch. In 1928, Hammond and Bispham were able to buy the White Grass back, and the ranch operated for many years until Frank Galey, Hammond's stepson, inherited and took over the ranch. He expanded it and ran it successfully until his death in 1985.

The Triangle X

Located across the highway from the old Cunningham Cabin historic site sits the Triangle X Ranch. In 1926, John S. Turner and his wife, Maytie, bought a homestead from Bill Jump and began operating it as a dude ranch. Just three

Corrals on the Triangle X

years later, in 1929, they sold to the Snake River Land Company but secured a lease to continue operating the ranch. Through various leases and heirs, the ranch kept operating, and today this concession is still run by the Turner family as the last of the old Jackson Hole dude ranches.

The STS Ranch

In 1914, a young Philadelphia socialite named Frances Mears stayed at the Bar BC Ranch, where she met a wrangler named Buster Estes. They married, and she was disowned by her family. In 1922, the couple was able to take over a seventy-six–acre tract just south of Moose. They built a small dude ranch by hand while Buster worked at the local sawmill (Sawmill Ponds on the Moose Wilson Road) and Frances sold fresh produce and food to tourists. They continued to enlarge and refine their business until the Great Depression in 1929. They leased a portion of the ranch, and when World War II began, they closed it while they worked in the war industries. In 1945, they sold the STS to the Muries—Olaus and Mardy, and Adolph and Louise. The Muries eventually sold the ranch to the National Park Service. Today it is maintained and run as a cooperative partnership between The Murie Center and the National Park Service.

The Double Diamond

Today's Climber's Ranch, a rustic hostel catering to mountaineers, began life in 1924 as the Double Diamond Ranch. It sat in a meadow at the base of the glacial moraine that contains Taggart Lake. Established in a partnership by local cowboy Frank Williams and Philadelphia dude Joseph Clark, the Double Diamond was built on forty acres purchased from homesteader James Manges. The two men opened it as a ranch for boys and drew their clientele largely from the Philadelphia area.

The Double Diamond was very successful for many years. Joseph Clark sold out in the late 1930s, and Frank Williams and his new partners continued to run the ranch until Williams died in 1964. His heirs sold to the National Park Service. A wildfire burned many of the original buildings in 1985.

The Flying V

This ranch began in 1928 when Jack and Dollye Woodman bought a 160-acre homestead at the mouth of Ditch Creek, on the present-day eastern boundary of the park. Named the Flying V, it was operated as a dude ranch until the Woodmans sold it in 1935, to mountain climbing guide Paul Petzoldt and one of his clients, Gustav Koven. They changed the name to the Ramshorn, and it operated through several changes of ownership until 1956, when the National Park Service bought it. In 1958, they leased it to Katie Starrat, who had operated a ranched called the Old Elbo since the 1940s. She renamed the Ramshorn the Elbo, and she ran it until she died in 1974. At that time, the NPS turned the use of the ranch over to the Teton Science School. Other buildings from the Elbo were eventually moved to the site, creating the present-day campus.

The Danny Ranch

The Danny Ranch, started in 1922 by Tony S. Grace on a 160-acre plot just east of String Lake, only operated for eight years. Grace sold to John D. Rockefeller Jr.'s Snake River Land Company in 1930, and his Teton Lodge Company renovated the buildings and ran it until the late 1930s. A 1935 fire destroyed the main house, but Tony Grace's residence was enlarged to form the present-day main lodge of the Jenny Lake Lodge. The ranch was named for Danny Strange, daughter of its original investor.

Tony S. Grace

HARRISON R. CRANDALL PHOTO

The Square G

Square G

NPS PHOTO

While technically not a dude ranch, the Square G was notable for its location near Jenny Lake. Homesteaded in 1927, it sat in the meadow not far from today's Cathedral Group scenic turnout. Albert and Lida Gabbey had housekeeping cabins, a dining lodge, a store, and a gas station. It was a popular site, and the Gabbeys ran it successfully until it was purchased for inclusion in Grand Teton National Park in 1951. The buildings were removed in 1956.

Looking Back

From the prehistoric people who lived here as the landscape thawed out from the last Ice Age to the homesteaders who first plowed the rocky earth and the National Park Service managers who have worked since 1929 to preserve the valley's natural and cultural features—all are part of the Tetons' human history.

As resident naturalist Olaus Murie wrote in the 1950s, "Jackson Hole is not merely a sky-piercing range of mountains … It is a country with a spirit. Those of us who have our homes here and are raising families can help interpret … the spirit of Jackson Hole, forged out of long controversy, tempered with our love for the valley."

This perspective seems relevant for all generations and races that have called this place home.

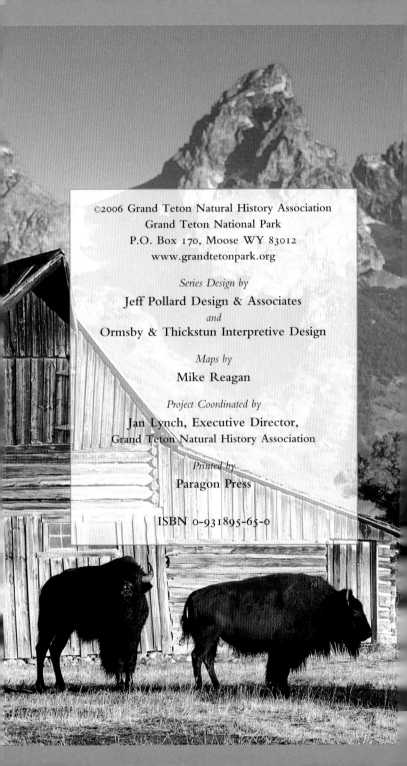

©2006 Grand Teton Natural History Association
Grand Teton National Park
P.O. Box 170, Moose WY 83012
www.grandtetonpark.org

Series Design by
Jeff Pollard Design & Associates
and
Ormsby & Thickstun Interpretive Design

Maps by
Mike Reagan

Project Coordinated by
Jan Lynch, Executive Director,
Grand Teton Natural History Association

Printed by
Paragon Press

ISBN 0-931895-65-0